HURON COUNTY LIBRARY

O9-BRZ-499

HURON COUNTY LIBRARY

2 008 184675 8

Date Due

JUN 11		
JUL 29		
AUG 17		
DEC 18		
Jun 2		
MAR 8		
OCT 19		
NOV 15		
NOV 27		
JUN 7		
APR 2		

BRODART, INC.   Cat. No. 23 233   Printed in U.S.A.

14664

819
.154
McKay

McKay, Don, 1942-
    Night fields : poems / by Don McKay. -- Toronto :
McClelland & Stewart, c1991.
    81 p.

    04743180   ISBN:0771057628 (pbk.)

    I. Title

6721   91APR17   06/go   1-00964570

ALSO BY DON MCKAY

Air Occupies Space   1973
Long Sault   1975
Lependu   1978
Lightning Ball Bait   1980
Birding, or desire   1983
Sanding Down this Rocking Chair on a Windy Night   1987

NIGHT FIELD

Poems by
DON McKAY

MAY 27 1991

-- : 14664

Copyright © 1991 Don McKay

All rights reserved. The use of any part of this
publication reproduced, transmitted in any form
or by any means, electronic, mechanical, photo-
copying, recording, or otherwise, or stored in a
retrieval system, without the prior written con-
sent of the publisher – or, in case of photocopy-
ing or other reprographic copying, a licence
from Canadian Reprography Collective – is an
infringement of the copyright law.

CANADIAN CATALOGUING IN PUBLICATION DATA

McKay, Don, 1942-
  Night field

Poems.
ISBN 0-7710-5762-8

I. Title.

PS8575.K28N53 1991 C811'.54 C90-095511-2
PR9199.3.M323N53 1991

The publisher makes grateful acknowledgement
to the Ontario Arts Council for its financial as-
sistance.

Set in Sabon by the Typeworks, Vancouver
Printed and bound in Canada by John Deyell Company

McClelland & Stewart Inc.
The Canadian Publishers
481 University Avenue
Toronto, Ontario M5G 2E9

For Jan

NIGHT FIELD

Don McKay

Contents

I

THE WOLF

Sleep, my favourite flannel shirt, wears thin, and shreds, and birdsong happens in the holes. In thirty seconds the naming of species will begin. As it folds into the stewed latin of afterdream each song makes a tiny whirlpool. One of them, zoozeezoozoozee, seems to be making fun of sleep with snores stolen from comic books. Another hangs its teardrop high in the mind, and melts: it was, after all, only narrowed air, although it punctuated something unheard, perfectly. And what sort of noise would the mind make, if it could, here at the brink? Scritch, scritch. A claw, a nib, a beak, worrying its surface. As though, for one second, it could let the world leak back to the world. Weep.

BLACK SPRUCE

Eventually the pack becomes
your hump, the weight of your food
and the weight of your clothing
and the weight of your shelter
and the weight of your forgetfulness of all
of the above.
        Added to the sad
dumb sadness of your ass as it tries
to reconstrue itself as muscle,
lift your life up,
over another ridge.

•

Forebodings,
aftermaths: beaches
rubbled with logs, the work
of giants with no patience, bugger this.
No one says Wendigo.
A suicidal river
strangled on the sand it vomited into its mouth,
still lying in its bed, unburied, shape of river
body of desert. A footbridge
smashed by runoff. Blue green green
blue water filter – and
refiltering the light into the welcome-
lonesome-spirit clarity of
icy depths, death by crystal.
Whatever it is that
reaches into whatever it is in us that
reaches into emptiness and resonates
until we recognize this common
chamber as an organ of ourselves.
Thirst.

•

Along the shoreline, shelves, soft
curves as the rock
erotically enters water. Shoulder
knuckle skull hip vertebreast combined and
recombined: three
hundred million years before the animals
appeared in the Triassic
they were dreamt of in Precambrian
volcanoes. Feel the muscle
slide over bone as you crouch
beside a Harebell, think of rootlets
reaching into rock, licking its slow
fury into food,
hoisting this small blue flag.

•

Third day out, the climbing I
thinks with the booming valves of its heart and loose-knit
clan of muscles with an ear out for the gimpy knee and

that particular downward twist which sets it
                              off whine whine
whining like a crabby aunt and though it's mostly on
                              descents we don't
take any chances, plant the walking stick a temporary
                              tree and

lean into the lift. To parachute
into the body, live its languages and get to know
                              exotic customs
and beliefs. Learn to plod. Converse through prunes,

moleskin, caladryl and tensor bandages. Coffee. If
                    Aunt Knee
goes wonky it will be the birth of melodrama on
                    For Whom
the Bell Tolls Ridge, you folks go on, just

leave me where I see the sun set, scratch the last
essential lyric on the rock. Did Hemingway
eat prunes? If the earth moves for two

people screwing does it stand still for the moose? Pause,
pant. You'd think Ontario would ban the
Lady's Slippers all along this trail with their beautiful

blowsy how-about-it-sailor blossoms and their
sexual deceit, the bee crawls in the front door,
where's the nectar, slips, can't get out she's

got to use the back, squeezes
under the stigma (leaving pollen) past
the anthers (local pollen catches in her hair) you have

to wonder what kind of mind thinks
all this (however slowly)
up. Pause, pant. One more

contour line. Susan still carrying the three-pound, hollowed
rock she picked up at White Gravel River, now
appreciating at a rate of, say

one helping jello instant pudding every day with interest
at two bites chocolate compounded hourly, let's see,
if she manages to get it home it will be priceless as for

instance, water. Yesterday we lost our way and then
Jan found a tiny flower with a bloom as complicated
as a snowflake, petals then meta-petals in a sort of
                              cross, Naked

Mitrewort, we pick it from the flower book to carry in our
                              heads with Pale
Corydalis, Bluebead Lily, Starflower, Butterwort,
Gay Wings. Dangerous bouquet says Tim. The spruce is
                              thinning out, hang

on Auntie, Red Pine growing singly seem to
radiate through trunks and needles like
sopranos opening into air unlike the

spruce still introspecting,
deepening their green as the climbing I and co.
hoist themselves onto belly-smooth red-brown rock,

swing off pack, catch water bottle, Lake Superior
                                        gleams and
flashes, here's to it, forty thousand of our
heartbeats in a single glance.

•

Head back, tail up,
total,
the Winter Wren empties itself in a
frenzy of riffs and trills.
Another song,
another run up to the edge.
I piss into a fat
cushion of moss,
thoughtful.
All around us spruce
distilling darkness out of sunlight,
cradling it in their arms.

Irresistible, on this atmospheric planet, where
there's a blue to carry the heart home and a blue
for virgins and a blue to call
the spider from the drain.
Nobody argues with its
shameless imitation of love, diving
simultaneously into the eye and out of sight: sea,
sky, the absence of convulsions and flags,
our own errata winking at us out of depths or heights.
Knowing that one day we will fall to black
or fade to grey, and blue
has been both places and includes them
as a saxophone includes its drastic
possibilities. It's with us.
We've been gone before.

ANOTHER THEORY OF DUSK

What is there to say
when the sky pours in the window
and the ground begins to eat its figures?
We sit like dummies in our kitchen, deaf
among enormous crumplings of light.
Small wonder each thing looms
crowding its edge.
In silent movies everyone overacts a little.

It would be nice to breathe the air inside the cello.
That would satisfy one
thirst of the voice. As it is

only your ribcage speaks for me now,
a wicker basket full of sorrow and wish, so tough
so finely tuned we have often
reinvented the canoe

and paddled off.
It would be nice to write the field guide for those riverbanks,
to speak without names of the fugitive
nocturnal creatures that live and die in our lives.

MEDITATION ON A GEODE

To find one, even among souvenirs of Banff from acrylic to zinc, is to realize that rock, ordinary limestone, composes in its own medium and has other lives. This one sits by the telephone, an impacted hollow whole note, formed, says my old geology textbook, from the modification and enlargement of an original void. O : every time I look inside, that twinge of tabu. And something more familiar: impossible words forming a lump in my throat, the petrified ovary of the unspoken.

I have been trying to respond to the spaces in your letter, its rests and lapses, and the slight halo effect of words spoken in an art gallery. Thanks especially for the potato salad recipe with the missing mystery ingredient. You've been breathing the spiked air of solitude and I'm feeling jealous. Echoless. Probably I should get more exercise, once upon a time, once upon a time. Meanwhile the geode by the phone. Astounded.

Once upon a time there was a little animal who lived and died, got buried in the silt and gradually decayed to nothing, which filled up with water. And on the inner surface of the hole a shell of jellied silica dividing the water inside, which is quite salty, from the fresher water outside in the limestone: a tiny ocean in an egg. In which a subtle and irresistible idea, osmosis, unclenches outward against the rock, widening the hole and seeping through the silica until the salts inside and outside balance. And everything (slow gong) crystallizes: : animal, emptiness, ocean, gland : ode of the earth.

OLD AUSABLE RIVER IN NOVEMBER

The canoe a ripe weight
cantilevered on my knees: this pause we know

in music and in love we taste it, a small wound
which the silence does not heal but instantly

converts to mouth
closing on a seed or fly.

Three weeks ago these leaves
would scatter down to float, upturned

Italian hands.
Now half-sunk, they are dead caresses

darkening toward the bottom.
We lean.

Introspective mirror, colour of the sky
before the day and night were separated,

it discloses, in overarching maple limbs,
the shy grace of the recently made naked.

He sits behind the wheel, scribbling. The old Phoenix gapes, its hood up and radiator out, toothless. All the way up Michigan and through the Sault the temp light has been winking its psychotic red eye, I've got a secret. Disputation, hermeneutics, *ratio,* apostasy, gestalt, internal combustion, dread: the energy accumulates. Now, sidelined, he is free to write a poem that visits the great shrines of sleep, easily coasting over the hassles of cashflow, Art will be back in an hour, and the national embarrassment of actually breaking down in Wawa, riding its seamless traffic, its eros of loss, the run-on sentence of the other world or the fifty thousand humilities of Lake Inferior, and this is not it but it is out there, animal, redundant, endless, and we can tell he is writing into it while we gnaw the time with those phone call coffee phone call who's got the aspirin asphalt coffee blues.

THE WOLF

Wolf: a jarring sound occasionally heard from certain notes in bowed instruments. The body of the instrument, as a whole, resonates to a certain note and jars, just as a room-ornament is sometimes found to jar every time a certain note of the piano is played.
—THE OXFORD COMPANION TO MUSIC

Poplar Grove is when the cello shakes the breastbone
and The Cage
is when the heart does.
Antelope is elongation of the field, when brain
has the illusion of unfolding into prairie.
Sometimes an acoustic host expects the melody so
eagerly a placeless humming "huhuhu" develops
and flies round among the *putti:*
This is the Snipe.
But The Wolf:
The Wolf is when the wood itself,
carved, bent, and
stretched, is moved –
perhaps some memory of rain –
and woofs its execrable music.
Then some of us will be embarrassed
and pretend it never happened, and the rest
will think of driving home after the sky has
snowed its first wet snow, then drizzled,
then turned so dark and glossy that the highway
                              dreams the
deep black lava dream and flows toward it,
asphalt to asphalt.

CHOOSING THE BOW

In the factory of lever and hinge
all poems begin with oil

•

Medicine stick, belly of earth, medicine stick, belly of earth

•

That an impulse travels shoulder-elbow-wrist and gathers (sensory redundance) in the fingertips has generally been assumed. Recently, however, the discovery of the dendritic aureole (the "moustache" or otter-awareness effect) has given rise to speculation that the fiddler experiences vestigial antennae like the phantom pain of amputated limbs and that her experience of muscular *déjà vu* is, as it were, thousands of absent *sensilla placodea* grieving for themselves.

•

The dark bow, you explain, wants her head and
flicks into saltando, taking arpeggia
the way a teenager takes stairs. The heavier,
reddish bow will bite and makes a crosshatched,
comfortable largo. In the kitchen
the violin-maker's daughter is pretending
she has lost her hands.
Where did they go?
Are they hiding under the snow, clasped,
plotting in their sleep like rhizomes?
Before the discovery of America,
her father says, bows were made of ironwood.
Now we use pernambuco, from Brazil,
a wood so dense it

tenses at the slightest flex
and sinks in water. Outside the window, snow
swoons abundantly into its soft self, as though
a great composer had stopped
dead in his tracks, spilling an infinity of crotchets
quavers phrases into the earth's lap.

You guess where did my hands go, o.k.?
Have they moved in
with the rabbits, to stroke their terrors
and teach them to count?
Or are they stealing secrets
from the spruce, the horse, the pernambuco,
maple, whale, ebony, elephant and cat
in order to compose themselves a voice?

Riversinew forming in the other room.

Someone knocking at the door.

Trying to think inside
its idiom no knife no fork and no
memento mori: "skull"
clobbers this
lighter-than-air variation
on the egg. Whoever lived here deftly
entered anonymity:
membrane of bone,
koan you could sit and write inside and then
go out to a movie (Hitchcock's comedy
"The Birds") and then come home and
fall asleep and dream the rite of spring and then
wake up and forget. Everyone
who reads would like to be read, sometime,
by the music. I have read or dreamt
that Indigo buntings in their nests
gaze into the stars and that the stars
gaze back into them,
mapping their language on each tiny roof.
Planetaria. This may be
the death of distance and its children.
If, like me,
you feel the urge to stick the sharp end
in your ear
(hoping for some
secret of the air)
be careful.
We are big and blunt and easily fooled and know few
of the fine points of translation.

DRIFTWOOD

Snap.
Not weightless but
participating in another gravity
unfelt by us.

We feed the fire.
Behind our backs, birch
glimmers, having gathered wind and moonlight
into itself.
Missipishiu, inland ocean
breathes against its rock, caress
erase, caress
erase

thought wearing thin
thinner
          window suddenly
flung open by a loon.

Great grandmother's blanched
bones catch fire   enter air.

II

THE DUMPE

BONE POEMS

I

Mind is crossed, above
by clouds, below
by their fallen brothers, the bears: brown, black
cinnamon and grizzly.
Busy as tugs
they tow their moods across the screen.

But body is the home of a birch wood
whose limbs are unwritten-upon paper, listening
motionless

full of dance

Of all your secret selves, it is the most remote, communi-
cating in the intimate, carrying timbre of glaciers and French
horns. Its unheard hum arrives at inner ear without passing
the receptionist. Mostly we are tuned to the heart (passion,
drugs, intrigues, attacks), but it is through the bone self that
the deaf hear symphonies, that mothers know beforehand
that their children are in trouble, and that we maintain our
slender diplomatic ties with the future and the dead. Bones
attend to deep earth, while your heart is learning, year by
year, to listen to your watch.

III

Outcrops. A lost
civilization hinted at by cheekbones.
Little is known, except
they knew how to be lost. Apparently
where we have closets
they had porches.
Everything blew off.
Experience was complete combustion, hence
the scarcity of ash or
personality:

their minds unstained glass
windows, delicately veined
as wings of dragonflies

IV

Antler

Holy Cow. Some creature
so completely music that its bones

burst into song.
Now we understand those stories of the savage

pianist, annually growing hands
that stretch three octaves reaching for the loon's cry fingers

sprouting from their fingers, brilliant
failures thrown out each December.

Truly, we will also lose ourselves in forest,
wearing our lawn rakes fanned above our heads, tines

turned toward its darkness,
listening for the lost arpeggio.

V

Vertebral Lament

More orders from the star chamber: Higher! Straighter!
To us, the once proud horizontal race of snakes.

Fuck their empire. Remember the amputation.
Recite the remnants of our alphabet, Atlas to Lumbar,

meditating on the lost ones. Query, Sylphid, Zeno,
how they listened and lashed the air and

taught us poetry and danced, far
lither than the arms of maestro as

attired in his pathetic morning coat
he writhes upon the podium.

VI

Now we know the price of x-ray:
if you want to see your bones you have to
flirt with death a little. Moon-bathe.
Anticipate their liberation from your flesh.

Once upon a time
shoe stores had peepshows that could
melt your skin and show the bones
inside your feet (plenty of room for him to grow there,
ma'am). You looked down zillions, back
into an ocean where a loose
family of fish was
wriggling in blue spooky light.

There are other worlds.
Your dead dog swims in the earth.

VII

One day you will have to give yourselves
to clutter and the ravages
of air and be
no good for nothing and forget
how de ankle connected to de shinbone and de
word of de lawd. Truthless
you will lie in the kingdom of parts among
Loosestrife, Nightshade,
Pokeweed.
You will learn the virtues of your former enemies,
the sticks and stones, and bless
the manyness of rain.
In some other lifetime you may work
as a knife, a flute, a pair of dice, a paperweight
or charm.
Meanwhile forgive the *rasp rasp*
of the teething wire-haired
terrier.

NOCTURNE MACDONALD-CARTIER FREEWAY

In the archipelago of coffee, each man is an island. The women are – who knows where – withdrawn but not quite vanished, like god at the end of the last century. Between your figure and the ground there is a tissue of airless space about the thickness of a piece of paper, in which all double helices untwine, adieu my little corkscrew, and swim offstage at the speed of light. Warnings, some visible, are posted at each junction. The floor may be slippery, the eyes in the mirror may be holes, the cashier may be unfamiliar with your gravity, the money may be avian. But the coffee is real and powers the economy.

Along the re-entry ramp the transports twinkle. Probably their drivers are asleep, ghosts in the machines. We say good-bye to Christmas in Cubism and follow our headlights into the dark.

We drive because we believe in the death of traffic. There will be a kitchen in the middle of a forest, its windows widening slowly, reaching their frames but continuing until the walls are erased. You turn on the tap, an underground river leaps sixty feet into your mouth, a perfectly composed dream. No phone-ins. No hits from the sixties. No eye in the sky. No internal combustion of any kind. No memory lane. The first song sparrow will have your whole head to itself.

THE DUMPE

*An old dance of which no one knows anything except that the
word is generally used in a way that suggests a melancholy
cast of expression.*

—THE OXFORD COMPANION TO MUSIC

No one remembers what is
danced to the echoless drum one

             one

             one

             one or you can simply
slam the door.
When you feel the spirit move you
plant your foot. Stamp each
butt into the pavement.
Close your right hand loosely
round a disconnected gear shift.
You never asked for this. This
is what you got. Forget
"refining figuration of the human
form in space" and other psychosomatic noise.
Wear your luggage.
Get in line.
Think of the alligator and the pig.
They never asked for this.
Drop the disembodied body. Stamp.
Forget.

NIGHT FIELD

i

"Burning thirty years of paper,"
he can't resist repeating to himself as he
tosses another shopping bag of correspondence on the fire.
Thirty Years of _____ (fill in the blank) gathers,
listens to some speeches, marches on the embassy and turns
ugly with the desire to let go and be mob, the air
a thick fabric of thuds. Already they have burnt
the library at Ephemeros, bills, receipts, notes on
notes on drafts of copies, tax data from 1978 and
                              an interesting,
well-written paper on one of the most difficult
problems in Spinoza, B +. In his daughter's art class
they did gesture drawings of a moving model on newsprint,
fifteen seconds a sketch, no more, and since
these are already two-thirds of the way to flux
they bloom at once, while the notebooks and journals
close themselves in airless strata.
So many styles of fury: he names the tickle and twist,
                              the Baked Alaska,
tongue-of-the-serpent, at one
point in the life of the fire it reads as we do,
one page at a time, but purely, lifting
and curling, then browning each leaf before –
nothing is cooking here –
the burst of perfect understanding.
Leaving only black flecks to float off and briefly
speckle the air. Junk food for bats, he thinks, or
echoes from that dreadful place, the blank page.
That pool full of wonderful risk.

The painting was given to him by his godparents a few years before his godmother died, a gesture so loaded it occupied his mind like a cathedral. In their tiny basement flat it had taken up a whole wall. Mostly black, but opening into a spectrum of purples and bronzes when you drew close, it had the force of an icon presiding over their collection of books and records, the splendid clutter of art spilling from shelves onto the floor, leaving only enough room for Marg to pass in her wheelchair. There is a tuft or tussock of straw in its lower middle, as though briefly caught in a headlight. He would sit, listening to The Trout or The Pastorale, staring at this tuft, imagining the truck (an old 40's pickup with a plywood box on the back) paused for those few seconds at the gateway to the field, then backing up and turning, the cone of light swinging in a short arc across the grass, then the velvet purple-black closing in entirely, an eclipse. His eye dawdling over the spray of straw, always aware of before and after, two unknowns. The painting like one frame in a long dark film.

Just before his mother had her heart operation, she was given a weekend pass from the hospital. And since he lived in the country close by, both his parents came to stay at his house. They all sat on the porch and talked gently. Seen through her eyes, everything was etched and precious: the afternoon unfolded itself.

But that night she had trouble with breathlessness and angina, and lay awake for a long while, staring at the painting on the wall opposite.
"I hate that painting," she said at breakfast.
"What, Marg's painting? Why?"

"It has a monster in it, like a death's head. It reminds me of everything that happened to Marg, that whole terrible business. It's like it's mocking us. Everything."

"I'll move it," he said, "but I've never seen anything like that and I've looked at that painting quite a bit. Where is this critter?"

"Right in that mess or bundle of whatever it is that's lit up. I know what you're thinking, but it's there all right, and once you see it you can't ignore it. I just stared and stared and felt worse and worse. Go look. There's a definite nose and this sneering mouth and a black pit for an eye. Terrible."

"That's just a bundle of grass, lit up by a flashlight or something, like you're walking in a field at night."

"Then it's a field with a monster in it," she said firmly.

He took down the painting, and looked for the monster. His father could see it, and so could others, once it was pointed out to them, but he never could. He often found himself gazing into the field while talking on the phone, tilting his head this way and that way, trying this or that combination of straws and blackness. Sometimes he does think "Rorschach test." Sometimes he thinks "coils and recoils of interpretation." And sometimes he feels like the inadequate hero of a fairy tale whose shape he can't make out: the old woman is an old woman, the dog is a dog, the field is a field, and the monster who will laugh and steal the silver thread of meaning from a life is never there when he's looking.

iii

The movers, having cursed their possessions,
cubed them in the van and left.
Now the hangers hang like queries in the closets,
the carpet runs unimpeded to the wall,
and the walls, freed from calendars and art, relax
into a gentle geometry of their own.
The house listens, surprised
to hear itself think.
He wishes he could listen with it, that he'd lived
less noisily among its shades and angles.
Maybe the house hears branches creaking in the forest
no one walks in. Scraps of aria under the eaves.
The dog whimpering in his sleep.

The sky looks elsewhere, embarrassed.
I have evidently wandered into an old regimental photograph and stand, fading, having no slang, in its legendary mud. We slouch at attention. It is still too wet for the machines, and it will always be. Our sweethearts have married the boys from two doors down and we forget why we were so sad and horny. After the ball is over in Hell Collegiate and Vocational School, no one tidies up, though everyone, mildly encumbered with crêpe, wishes someone would. Wasn't there some magic word that could translate sunlight into sugar? Our tongues stiffen. We all worry at once, cackling like old plastic raincoats over the death of the angel, the death of the author, the breakdown of the tractor. (There was a time, now.) How long until we're rumours of the death of death? Until we always, only, occur in public?

MOTH FEAR

These must be the dead souls who have not
quite graduated into ghosts, air
which has barely begun to curdle.
No wonder they're terror-stricken, still
clinging to the light, indentured
to the dark, flapping the loose
bandage of themselves against the screen.
Why can't desire just die and be dead
when we are?
Let them in
they collapse upon your charity
eat your socks and drown themselves
in coffee cups.
Crush them
they find their voices in your memory.
Better not.

It is possible to feel awful and
unserious, to be trapped in the comic strip edition
of *King Lear*. The band keeps playing
flatter and flatter until
flatness gathers, wisps become clouds, then
tears I never wept return as
voices lapping
          could be the sea
          could be the zoo
          could be the ambi-guest who
makes yerself at herm
curdles into yer ermchair
mashes yer suet
simpers.

The budget for this horror movie is so low the ghosts
are mildewed pillows and the haunted house
is my old shed full of domestic rejects, tangled
hoses, tires from forgotten cars, bicycle bones, three
sofas stacked like Frank Lloyd Wright for rabbits, Fusty,
Musty, Cottontail and Peter, who have
moved incestuously in. Sinister
ex-tools and toys, grey with dead
utility and fun.
Antipollen.

Arrivederci Trauma: it's
dependable Inertia who has nursed us,
unnoticed as a handkerchief, now
the handkerchief in this ancient family sitcom

worn down to its plastic tubing and bald all-purpose
indoor-outdoor carpet, rolled up in the corner with
                              the rusty
rake, the croquet set, the cat cage.

Familiar townships: shelter, geranium,
the bottleneck, the panhandler, fast food,
the happy hunting ground, supreme soviet,
the handkerchief. In aerial photos
suburbs curlicue from the city's rough
geometry. Once in a story with a wise
old gardener there lived a snake
named Dave. We too
wish to believe in rituals performed on floodlit
diamonds in the township of the perfect game.

Through poetry and other savage
poignancies we glimpse
the hinterland – a group of moons
with pockets, Karst topographies inscribed with streamless
valleys, sinkholes, caves, and disappearing
rivers. No one lives there
yet the rock is rich with loss.
Something funny happens in paused
cadence. Lurch,
sudden turbulence the past slops forward
with its knaves and wolves still
scavenging abandoned picnics. Somehow
we grow the animals we need, cunning, watchful,
cowardly, with the survivor's
sidelong grace.

MEDITATION ON SHOVELS

How well they love us, palm and instep, lifeline
running with the grain as we
stab   pry   heave
our grunts and curses are their music.
What a (stab) fucking life, you dig these
(pry) dumb holes in the ground and (heave) fill
them up again until they (stab)
dig a fucking hole for you:
                              beautiful,
they love it, hum it as they stand,
disembodied backbones,
waiting for you to get back to work.

But in the Book of Symbols, after Shoes
(Van Gogh, Heidegger, and Cinderella)
they do not appear.
Of course not.
                    They're still out there
humming
patiently pointing down.

III

METAXU

LUKE & CO.

i

Shriek of brakes spiked
with your spirit splits the evening suddenly
this is it   everything leaks   we draw heavy
outlines trying to keep stone stone
boot boot shovel shovel
shovel this raw mouth into the earth
and feed you to the meadow.

ii

Each time he settled on his blue-black sofa Luke
went out, invisible except for small white patches
on his chest, left forepaw and the tiny paint-brush
tufts on his tail and prick-sack, winking when he
wagged or
          recomposed his curl:
milkweed
growing on this wild unspecial
patch of ground
            let your silk slip
            gently   to the wind.

iii

A dog on his sofa, a dog
underground, a committee of dogs which
circulates beyond the bounds of decency
sniffing crotches
raiding garbage
stealing from the butcher
begging from the banker
befriending nasty Mrs. Kuhn, convincing folk
that every act is sexual and droll.
                              Raggedly
they range the meadow,
alternate hosts for all our seminal ideas
(soft sell, the revolving
door, the interminable
joke) tucked in snug cocoons behind their wise
unknowing eyes:
                    underground
          they spread contagiously, freelancing dreamlife to
          dreamlife through networks of long rambling after-
          dinner anecdotes   Mr Glover had an old blind
          terrier could fetch a ball by listening to it hit
          and roll, I don't know, could be he smelt it in
          the air   sure well Luke followed his nose the
          way Ezekiel followed God, he'd vacuum up your
          trail like you had fishline paying out your arse
          you'd double back it didn't matter he would find
          you up a tree   thing is, like they only partly
          live in this dimension since they smell and hear
          things that do not exist for us so on their level
          its like synesthesia is common sense   well you
          know Alice Dragland had such ears folks said her
          mother was part fruit bat she would practise

flying when the family was asleep and when she
swam (for miles) behind the boat she mostly sailed
and then of course there's breakthroughs
                                        as when Luke
discovered down-filled pillows and extrapolated,
grazing the surface of soft
improbable objects with exquisite
fish-bites, *chien stupide, chien*
brillant, trying to tease feathers
from the cat the sofa and at least one
English professor of each rank and gender,
chien comme une tasse de la nuit, he wouldn't
let himself become embossed with discipline
but played it like a melody
(Perdido Blues) from which he improvised in long
irregular loops
                    exits
entries. Letting him out in out to chase a
car bike jogger snowplow (caught, tossed in an
otter's arc of snow) rabbit motorcycle train the wind
whose speed
was with him even in repose a space
left in his dogginess for metamorphosis and style
where once
                    right here in this kitchen, Luke ate
                    three-fifths of Hemingway's *For Whom*
                    the Bell Tolls, fell asleep on his sofa
                    wrapped in the perfect fur sleeping bag
                                        of himself.

Among gaskets, couplings, fasteners, the bricoleur is brows-
ing in his favourite store, wearing that smudged, obviously
elsewhere expression, pregnant. Once again he is imagining
his way home by an unlikely set of islands. Back in his kitch-
en, there are shelves made of broken hockey sticks frankly
stating

> KOHO
>
> SHERWOOD
>
> GLASS STIFF
>
> VICTORIAVILLE

while they tote the cookbooks
and renounce the hook the spear the slash. Down the
plughole of the bathtub, like its inverted thought-balloon,
there is a congenial underworld of horned rats and adven-
ture. As he fingers the U-bolts, the bricoleur is probably
working on another form of kinship to dismay the anthropol-
ogists. Perhaps he will convert a chicken coop or reconceive
the bunk-beds as an Escher print of stairways and hide-outs.
A larynx for the wind made of doorskin and guitar strings sits
in our window humming horizon notes. A carved sumac to-
tem with two penises lounges on the 1949 edition of the En-
cyclopedia Britannica. Prairie elevators turn up in Ontario as
gravity-feed birdseed dispensers. There are songs full of vege-
tables and chance. "Got to meander if you want to get to
town." He lives by creeks. Invents them.

Speak gently of Poplar, who has
incompletely metamorphosed out of flesh
and still recalls the Saturday night
bath and toughly tender country blues which,
when she used to travel,
moved her.
Consider that her leaves are hearts,
sharpened and
inverted into spades. Who else
has strength to tremble,
tremble and be wholly trepid,
to be soft so she can listen hard,
and shimmer, elegant and humble,
in the merest wisp of wind?
Who blurs the brittle
creek bank, lisping into spring?
Who feeds the beaver, living in their culture
as potato lives in Irish? Well,
if a man begin to wonder in his tracks and
at them, arrowing behind him and before, should purpose
slow, grow empty arms,
and know itself again as slough or delta, then
that sometime man may wish for a chair of
                                    comprehending wood
to lay his many bones in: Poplar.

PLANTATION

i

Full moon and half a bottle. Silver maples
glimmer, white pine

retransmit the stars in tiny pin-
pricked constellations – the Toothbrush,

the Fly, the Dispersed
Porcupine. Out there

the shaved patient medicated
reshaved southern Ontario fieldscape

waits for something to be done to it
again. Years ago

pressing seedlings into meadow
I imagined something various and hairy,

habitat. Now
among such sharpness I negotiate a slow

dissolve to dark, drinking against the moon's white
mouth, getting drunk

by the deep shadows of my trees.

ii

November wind with its seductions –
every place it passes through

forgets to cling.
Each ash leaf

loosens,
half a clap

silently completed on the ground.
Inertia inside motion

as the stone
inside the cherry: I stand

handful of seed outstretched
waiting for the black-capped

nothing-at-all to flirt up
perch on my finger: pause: one

two three sixty-
fourth notes: off

quickness of air, Billie
Holiday

        lend me your ear
and I will listen down the falling

cadence of my spine
into my boots and through

putting down roots in the difficult
recycled soil of Lobo township.

MEDITATION ON SNOW CLOUDS APPROACHING THE
UNIVERSITY FROM THE NORTH-WEST

One of us, paused between buildings,
will remark that snow is the postmodern
medium, or national equivalent to Lethe,
and release us to our offices
and tweeds.
We are not
a simple people and we fear
the same simplicities we crave.
No one wants to be a terminal
Canadian or existentialist or child, dumbly
moved because the clouds are bruises,
crowskin coats through which invisible
bits of rainbow nearly break.

The clouds look inward, thinking of a way
to put this. Possibly
dying will be such a pause:
the cadence where we meet a bird or animal
to lead us, somehow,
out of language and intelligence.

DOMESTIC ANIMALS

that blue
blush rising in the snow and the dog

follows his nose into a drift: woof :   weightless
explosion on the moon. Farther off

the dead express themselves
in little lifts of painless terror. Unadulterated

dance. By the edge of woods
they dress and undress mindlessly

shopping, trying on snowsuits
bedclothes, elegant underwear, nothing

fits their windscape.
They'd rather be naked.

Who wouldn't?
                    Dutifully

we chase the news. We cook
and type. We

calibrate.
Our jobs are on the line, our speed

is Zeno's car. The same sunset
blooms, fades,

blooms, pursued from one horizon
to the next   while sleep

widens its sweet toothless
exit underneath the chair :   the missing

person :   the cat's own
ecological niche.

SONG FOR THE RESTLESS WIND

The wind is struggling in her sleep, comfortless
because she is a giant,

which is not her fault. Whose idea was it
to construct a mind exclusively of shoulders?

In her dream
the car chase always overtakes the plot and wrecks it.

Maybe she will wake up
a Cecropia moth, still struggling

in a kimono of pressed-together dust
bearing the insignia of night.

Or as her own survivor, someone
who felt that huge wrench

clamped to her skull, loosening cutlery and books,
whirling round her,

corps de ballet, then
exit every whichway,

curtain.

SONG FOR WILD PHLOX

Suddenly, June 1, for no good reason,
the riverbank opens its heart: purple,
purplish, blue, whitish, common
currency from a country warmer than ours,
but cooler in its evenings and foothills.
My Great
Aunt Helen, though proper, used to be addicted
to lacrosse, and sat behind the penalty box
to scold opposing players sent off. Nothing
we ever did deserves
these weeds, which seed themselves
in places we have honoured with neglect.
One evening the dog comes home
freckled with petals of phlox, and for a moment
I imagine the wild wedding in the meadow
where his ample humour must have fit right in
with its numerous kisses and pranks.

RECIPE FOR DIVERTIMENTO IN D, K: 136

1. *Allegro*

Gather tictocks, stir in a pot and feed to
tigers. Run these cats round a tree until they
turn to butter. Spread on a muffin. Makes an
excellent breakfast.

2. *Andante*

Let the clock remember the summer sadly.
Simmer. Tie this phrase to the seagull soaring
past. When seagull reaches the far horizon
lower the curtain.

3. *Presto*

Catch two chipmunks. Marinate. Open sleeping
clock and toss in merrily. Add the gusto.
Keep the sneezing regular, duple, hearty.
Tickles the angels.

Skinny music: needle
in its empty groove.
Our cattail torches make dark
darker but more interested in us,
gathered in velvet fists around each
halo of light. Slow
flits; we circulate as cautious
ceremonious bats.
                        Some, turning
with crossovers chick
chick chick place themselves
among the starswirl and the mix
of elements, as ice
receives the image of our torches deep within itself
and thinks.
Some may glimpse a lost one
in the spaces between skaters or the watchers,
elderly or pregnant,
by the bonfire.
And some may concentrate on carving little
crescents of this hospitable dark to carry home
and dwell on through the solitudes of daily,
perfectly legible, life.

WHITEOUT: FOR THE FALLEN POPLARS

Half-woke because the dog was whimpering
and scratching at the door and heard

a version of what he heard:
pressure,

a dream of deafness. Woke three-quarters. Skimmed
light. If the moon had a moon

poverty might be as famous as love: Honeymoon hôtel-
dieu. Then the first bone-shriek and I was

swimming to the window: milk and softness, *essence
de la famille* which fell on the unseen, unfallen

leaves. Another crack, rush
crash from the direction of the poplars and I overshot,

woke into that moment when the light becomes opaque
and floods the frame

and has weight.

NOSTRA

Noster, nostrum, nostra: "our." The term "nostrum" for a patent medicine derives from salesmen referring to "our drug."

When pain needs rest
it lies down in the bones
and dreams up fresh surprises, o its repertoire of style
exceeds New York. Its rhythms
cover everything between the Caribbean
and the Royal Bank, its ear
improves with age.
Unwritten fugues and
scherzi, ova, always foreign,
always ours. The super-spouse,
it knows us better than we know ourselves,
conducts us, like conscripted tourists,
to exotic places not usually open to the public. Pain,
the pure technician. Each performance,
say the critics, heartless and perfect, the precise
appassionata. When I breathe,
when I bend, when I laugh. Pain,
which takes us to the edge of being human and
throws up the blind.
And nothing is ever there.

•

No human being, Simone Weil declares,
should be deprived of *metaxu* – creature comforts
(home, country, culture) which allow
the spirit to persist without the superhuman cost
and benefit of sainthood. So:
these ways of naming pain in poetry
part A.S.A., part judo,
help us to digest the news
and take a portion of its energy
to warm a corner or a niche.
To sing the blues until they turn
metaxu: everyone can use
a little something

> till I get back on my feet
> till the winter leaves my limbs
> till I learn to live without her
> till I find some peace of mind
> till I get my act together
> till we gather at the river
> till the fever's gone forever
> till I get a little sleep.

•

The wrong rough road up to the trail head, washouts, boulders, no place to turn round, look this has to get us there eventually, as we slow see-saw through another washout, edge past another fallen tree, and are suddenly out of the forest into clearcut. We drive into its grief, our spiffy red truck I-think-I-canning through the burnt stumps and slash. Too much raw sky. And right in the middle, that strange encampment: a huddle of camper vans and tarps with a few people in lawnchairs sitting beside a stream that rushes, one live tongue, down the slope. Far-out baptists maybe, or a sect of anti-tourists soaking up the atmosphere. We kept on driving, finally did reach the trail head, saw some Calypso orchids, a moose, and a pair of Barrow's Goldeneye, the heroes of our postcards.

Later on we found that wrong road dotted on a more detailed map. And there, marked with a small x beside it, the word "Hotsprings." Ever since, my memory of that rag-tag encampment has been growing, shack by shack, beginning with a cardboard sign, THE LAST RESORT, tacked up on a charred stump by some terminal smartass. The memory's sky, which has obviously been painted on, is about 800 feet up and sagging badly. Ragged bits of it detach at intervals to cronk and wheel: ravens. No sheriff, no bad guys, nothing to steal. As we zoom in, we see that the place is really a sort of guano island made of empty bottles, boxes, and tubes of snake oil, gargling oil, wizard oil, Bromo Seltzer, aspirin, anacin excedrin tylenol, Lydia Pinkham's Vegetable Compound cured my female weakness, Kickapoo Sagwa and Indian Salve, Dr. Redwing's Mexican Herbs of Joy for heart disease, diabetes, piles, debility and bad complexion, vitamin E, after only 30 days wearing Dr. Dye's Voltaic Belt I experienced the complete restoration of manhood, Nuxated Iron, You May Have

a Tapeworm Up To 60 Feet Long, mandrake, Coricidin, Dr. Bell's Witch Hazel and Cucumber Cream, Epsom Salts, All Bran saved my marriage. Here and there trusses, pads, braces, girdles, strewn like failed pterodactyls. Through the barrio a figure, slowly coming into focus, drags a stone boat, on which we see a large amorphous lump, a potato from outer space, with knobs protruding like grudges or knees without limbs. It is, of course, myself. How long have I been dragging my body to the spa, toiling through this ruined forest, look at me, all skin and bone and nary a thought-balloon to my name. Other pilgrims, picked out in stark, still images, carry their bodies in plastic garbage bags (cut to: badly collapsed lawnchair) or push and roll them like lumpy pillows. Down the last logging road, laddered with bulldozer tracks (cut to: empty application form), down to the river whose water smells like sorrow, intimate, exotic, this is the water that has been there, fell on the mountain-
side and flowed on
downward into earth and kept on
trickling downward to its furnace, boiled, got
percolated up again like coffee, poured through the
backstreets of the cities of the windowless
empires of rock, washed its gravity and stole its
secrets, sulphur, calcium, potassium,
plutonium it gathers character and comes up
bubbling like a bath fart, this is the stream that speaks
arthritis, chilblain, dread, the eros that
embraces its decay I'm going to let my
bones go swimming with their kinfolk going to
let my carcass tell its troubles to the earth.

·

Nightmares that defect from sleep
and actually happen: should you set
the clock radio, carelessly
exactly on the hour, you may surface,
a Common Loon,
into the oil spill.
Two bars of insect music name the race
most likely to survive, and segue
into the upper case baptism of events:
estimated casualties   among the dead
officials fear
                some poisoned
                some in pieces, some
                on fire, all
shadowless and valuable as stocks and bonds, chauffeured,
coached into publicity by the
King James version of voice.

No more marshy metamorphosis for them.
Already they know how to wave rhetorically
and float their smiles like styrofoam.
Already they ignore the child who shouts inside
                                your head Where
are they taking you Why don't you listen, mouths
that widen into empty slots the entry to the underground
parkade and you must rise and dress and drive and
park and find the bodies they've left
lying on the concrete gather them into your trunk and
bring them back to bury in the humble
compost they should never have forsaken, home.

•

The day I pinned the diaper and my
left thumb to my son's right hip
there was silence for the space of one large
heartbeat while I realized that everything
was not o.k., for black
invisible fish had swum into his pupils
and begun to trouble the waters.
                                        Tribal
concentration: Man Pins Self To Son,
with close-up photos of two safety-pin pricks
one-half inch apart.

Into such a moment, say the legends,
laughter woke
and recognized the instruments of pain
and stole them, making his escape
by falling out a window.
Later on he loaned them to the dog,
whose own best-
friendliness was also tipped to the oblique —
fierce with savage ancestry.

•

So much that refuses to be written or
unwritten, won't
make up your mind. That
moment in the life of every headache
when lucidity approaches
and withdraws: fine points
stand within your vision but
outside your grasp, declining to visit
or rent the attic. Well,
who wants to live with trolls
befouling the bathroom and
banging their pans through the orchestra
when they're supposed to be locked up in the mountains?

But the mountains are full of raw talent.
Silently they breathe it into ordinary air to
writhe and die and
fall on the upper slopes as snow
: the place we long for and can't live.

•

Elders, wise ones, rode
the black horse of their hunger.
Some pain that isn't suffering, some place
it opens and receives the song.

Imagine them in woven
huts like baskets upside down, as though
caged by larger animals. The light
thinned down to flecks, the wind
to whistles. Music and chemistry of spruce.
Only the days and nights are eaten,
slowly. Beings
slip from human supervision and the great chain. Sleep and
                              waking
finally parley. Gifts are exchanged: a blanket,
a child.
        Medicine.
            Thoughts
that pass through language as the sun through water.

                          •

Let the snow fall gently past the mountain's face.
Lace brings out your bones.

Let the snow fall gently past the mountain's face.
Silent movies of forgetfulness.

Let the snow fall gently past the mountain's face.
I miss my dog. Together we were purely creature.

Let the snow fall gently past the mountain's face.
Take saxifrage, beardtongue, stonecrop.

Let the snow fall gently past the mountain's face.
Whisper into the lake.

Some of these poems have appeared in the following publications: *The Malahat Review, Arc, Descant, Saturday Night, The Canadian Forum, The Third Macmillan Anthology,* and *Kitchen Table Broadsides* No. 1. As always, thanks to friends and editors across the kitchen table, especially Jan Zwicky, Kim Maltman, Roo Borson, Tim Lilburn, and Stan Dragland.

A number of these poems are written with individuals in mind: "Another Theory of Dusk" is for Jan Zwicky; "Art's Auto Rad" is for Tim Lilburn; "Canadian Tyre" is for Stan Dragland; and "Night Skating on the Little Paddle River" is in memory of Bob Zwicky.